EMMANUEL JOSEPH

The Digital Dialectic, How Philosophy and History Inform the Age of Technology

Copyright © 2025 by Emmanuel Joseph

All rights reserved. No part of this publication may be reproduced, stored or transmitted in any form or by any means, electronic, mechanical, photocopying, recording, scanning, or otherwise without written permission from the publisher. It is illegal to copy this book, post it to a website, or distribute it by any other means without permission.

First edition

This book was professionally typeset on Reedsy.
Find out more at reedsy.com

Contents

1. Chapter 1: The Dawn of Technological Thought — 1
2. Chapter 2: The Philosophical Roots of the Digital Age — 3
3. Chapter 3: The Historical Context of Technological Evolution — 5
4. Chapter 4: The Symbiotic Relationship between Philosophy and... — 7
5. Chapter 5: The Role of History in Technological Development — 9
6. Chapter 6: The Ethical Dimensions of Digital Technology — 11
7. Chapter 7: The Impact of Technology on Human Identity — 13
8. Chapter 8: The Philosophical Implications of Artificial... — 15
9. Chapter 9: The Intersection of Technology and Society — 17
10. Chapter 10: The Future of Technology and Human Civilization — 19
11. Chapter 11: The Role of Education in the Digital Age — 21
12. Chapter 12: The Ethical Challenges of Biotechnology — 23

1

Chapter 1: The Dawn of Technological Thought

In the dawn of human civilization, the seeds of technological thought were sown. From the rudimentary tools of the Stone Age to the sophisticated mechanisms of ancient Greece and Rome, our ancestors displayed an innate ingenuity that laid the groundwork for the technological marvels we witness today. Philosophers like Thales and Aristotle pondered the nature of existence and the mechanics of the natural world, prompting early technological innovations. These early thinkers laid a philosophical foundation that intertwined with the burgeoning technological landscape, fostering a symbiotic relationship between thought and invention.

As we transitioned from the ancient to the medieval era, the philosophical inquiries of the time continued to shape technological advancements. The Scholastic thinkers of the Middle Ages, such as Thomas Aquinas, grappled with the nature of knowledge and the divine, indirectly influencing the development of technological thought. Their pursuit of understanding the natural world through a theological lens led to innovations in fields like astronomy, agriculture, and engineering. This era marked a critical juncture where philosophy and technology began to merge, setting the stage for the Renaissance and the scientific revolution that would follow.

The Renaissance, often regarded as the rebirth of classical knowledge, saw a resurgence in the study of ancient texts and an explosion of technological innovation. Figures like Leonardo da Vinci epitomized the fusion of philosophy and technology, as his inventions were deeply rooted in his philosophical understanding of nature and the human body. The printing press, invented by Johannes Gutenberg, revolutionized the dissemination of knowledge, making philosophical and technological ideas accessible to a broader audience. This democratization of knowledge catalyzed an era of unprecedented technological progress, driven by philosophical inquiry and human curiosity.

As the Renaissance gave way to the Enlightenment, the relationship between philosophy and technology grew even more intertwined. Enlightenment thinkers like Descartes, Locke, and Kant challenged traditional notions of reality, knowledge, and human potential. Their philosophical explorations spurred technological advancements, as inventors and scientists sought to translate abstract ideas into tangible innovations. The Industrial Revolution, fueled by Enlightenment principles, transformed society through the mechanization of production, transportation, and communication. This era marked a profound shift in human history, where the convergence of philosophy and technology began to reshape the world in ways previously unimaginable.

2

Chapter 2: The Philosophical Roots of the Digital Age

The digital age is not merely a product of technological innovation but also a culmination of centuries of philosophical inquiry. The Enlightenment era, with its emphasis on reason, empiricism, and individualism, laid the intellectual groundwork for the digital revolution. Philosophers like Immanuel Kant and John Locke questioned the nature of knowledge, perception, and reality, prompting a shift towards a more rational and scientific worldview. This philosophical shift provided the foundation for the development of computational theories and the eventual birth of digital technology.

In the 20th century, the advent of digital technology was deeply influenced by the philosophical principles of logic and computation. Alan Turing, often regarded as the father of computer science, was profoundly influenced by the works of philosophers like Bertrand Russell and Ludwig Wittgenstein. Turing's exploration of the limits of computation and artificial intelligence was rooted in his philosophical understanding of logic and the nature of the mind. His contributions laid the foundation for the digital age, where the boundaries between human thought and machine intelligence continue to blur.

The digital age has also been shaped by existential and postmodern philosophies that question the nature of identity, reality, and technology's impact on society. Philosophers like Jean-Paul Sartre and Michel Foucault explored the implications of technology on human existence and social structures. Their ideas resonate in contemporary debates about the ethical, social, and political implications of digital technology. As we navigate the complexities of the digital age, these philosophical inquiries remain crucial in understanding the broader implications of technological progress and its impact on humanity.

Moreover, the digital age has prompted new philosophical questions about the nature of consciousness, artificial intelligence, and the ethics of technology. The rise of AI and machine learning has raised profound ethical dilemmas about privacy, autonomy, and the potential for technological singularity. Philosophers like Nick Bostrom and Luciano Floridi are at the forefront of these discussions, exploring the ethical and existential challenges posed by advanced digital technologies. As we continue to advance technologically, the interplay between philosophy and technology remains a vital discourse, guiding us through the ethical and existential challenges of the digital age.

3

Chapter 3: The Historical Context of Technological Evolution

The evolution of technology is deeply intertwined with the historical context in which it develops. Each technological breakthrough is a reflection of the social, economic, and political conditions of its time. The Industrial Revolution, for example, was not only a period of significant technological advancement but also a time of profound social and economic change. The invention of the steam engine and mechanized production methods transformed industries and societies, leading to urbanization, shifts in labor patterns, and the rise of new social classes. This historical context highlights the interconnectedness of technology and society, where technological advancements drive and are driven by broader historical forces.

The 20th century witnessed unprecedented technological progress, fueled by the two World Wars and the Cold War. The demands of warfare and the subsequent arms race spurred innovations in various fields, from aviation and nuclear technology to computing and telecommunications. The development of the internet, initially a military project, eventually revolutionized communication and information sharing on a global scale. This period of technological evolution was marked by a complex interplay of political tensions, economic competition, and scientific curiosity, shaping the trajectory of technological progress.

The historical context of technological evolution also includes the social and cultural impact of technology on human life. The rise of mass media, for instance, transformed the way people consumed information and entertainment, influencing public opinion, cultural norms, and societal values. The advent of digital technology and the internet has further accelerated these changes, creating a hyperconnected world where information flows rapidly and effortlessly. Understanding the historical context of technological evolution provides insights into the broader societal implications of technological advancements and the ways in which technology shapes and is shaped by human history.

As we look to the future, the historical context of technological evolution serves as a reminder of the cyclical nature of technological progress. Each era of technological innovation brings new opportunities and challenges, shaped by the unique historical conditions of the time. The digital age, with its rapid advancements in AI, biotechnology, and quantum computing, presents both unprecedented possibilities and existential risks. By examining the historical context of technological evolution, we can better navigate the complexities of the present and future, informed by the lessons of the past.

4

Chapter 4: The Symbiotic Relationship between Philosophy and Technology

Philosophy and technology have always been in a symbiotic relationship, each influencing and shaping the other. Philosophical inquiries into the nature of existence, knowledge, and ethics have often driven technological innovations. Conversely, technological advancements have prompted new philosophical questions and debates. This dynamic interplay between philosophy and technology is evident throughout history, from the early mechanistic philosophies of the Enlightenment to contemporary debates about artificial intelligence and digital ethics.

One of the most significant examples of this symbiotic relationship is the development of artificial intelligence (AI). Philosophers like René Descartes and Gottfried Wilhelm Leibniz laid the groundwork for AI with their exploration of the nature of consciousness and the mechanics of thought. Their ideas about the mind as a machine capable of logical reasoning influenced the development of early computational theories and the eventual creation of intelligent machines. Today, AI continues to raise profound philosophical questions about the nature of consciousness, the ethics of machine intelligence, and the future of human-technology interactions.

The ethical implications of technology have been a central concern of philosophers throughout history. The rapid advancements in digital technology have brought new ethical challenges, from data privacy and cybersecurity to the impact of automation on employment. Philosophers like Hannah Arendt and Jürgen Habermas have explored the ethical and social dimensions of technology, emphasizing the need for critical reflection and ethical responsibility in technological development. Their insights remain crucial in guiding the ethical use of technology in the digital age.

Furthermore, the digital age has sparked new philosophical debates about the nature of reality and virtual existence. The rise of virtual reality (VR) and augmented reality (AR) technologies has challenged traditional notions of reality and perception. Philosophers like Jean Baudrillard and David Chalmers have explored the implications of these technologies on our understanding of reality, identity, and the self. As VR and AR become more integrated into our daily lives, these philosophical inquiries will continue to shape our perception and use of technology.

5

Chapter 5: The Role of History in Technological Development

History plays a crucial role in shaping the development of technology. Each technological innovation is a product of its historical context, reflecting the social, economic, and political conditions of its time. The printing press, for example, emerged during the Renaissance, a period of intellectual and cultural revival that demanded new means of disseminating knowledge. Similarly, the development of the internet was influenced by the military and scientific needs of the Cold War era. Understanding the historical context of technological development provides valuable insights into the forces driving innovation and the impact of technology on society.

The Industrial Revolution is a prime example of how historical conditions shape technological development. The economic demands of the time, driven by the rise of capitalism and the need for efficient production methods, spurred innovations in machinery and manufacturing processes. The steam engine, the spinning jenny, and other industrial inventions transformed industries and societies, leading to urbanization, changes in labor patterns, and the rise of new social classes. This period of technological development was deeply intertwined with broader historical forces, highlighting the interconnectedness of technology and history.

The 20th century witnessed rapid technological advancements, driven by the historical context of global conflicts and competition. The two World Wars and the subsequent Cold War spurred innovations in fields such as aviation, nuclear technology, and computing. The development of the internet, initially a military project, eventually revolutionized communication and information sharing. This period of technological development was marked by a complex interplay of political tensions, economic competition, and scientific curiosity, shaping the trajectory of technological progress.

As we look to the future, the historical context of technological development remains relevant. The digital age, with its rapid advancements in AI, biotechnology, and quantum computing, presents new opportunities and challenges. By examining the historical context of technological development, we can better understand the broader implications of technological progress and navigate the complexities of the present and future.

6

Chapter 6: The Ethical Dimensions of Digital Technology

The rise of digital technology has brought new ethical challenges that require careful consideration and critical reflection. The proliferation of data and the increasing capabilities of artificial intelligence raise profound ethical questions about privacy, autonomy, and the potential for technological harm. Philosophers and ethicists have been at the forefront of these discussions, exploring the ethical implications of digital technology and advocating for responsible and ethical use.

One of the most pressing ethical issues in the digital age is data privacy. The vast amounts of data collected by digital technologies, from social media platforms to smart devices, raise concerns about surveillance, consent, and the potential for misuse. Philosophers like Michel Foucault have explored the implications of surveillance and the loss of privacy in a digital society. Their insights highlight the need for robust data protection measures and ethical guidelines to safeguard individual privacy and autonomy.

Artificial intelligence also presents significant ethical challenges, particularly in areas such as bias, accountability, and the potential for harm. The use of AI in decision-making processes, from hiring to law enforcement, raises concerns about fairness, transparency, and the potential for discrimination. Philosophers like John Rawls and Martha Nussbaum have explored the ethical principles of justice and fairness, providing a framework for addressing these challenges. Their ideas emphasize the importance of ethical considerations in the development and deployment of AI technologies.

The ethical dimensions of digital technology extend to broader societal and environmental impacts. The increasing reliance on digital technologies raises questions about the digital divide, access to technology, and the potential for social and economic inequalities. Additionally, the environmental impact of digital technologies, from energy consumption to electronic waste, requires ethical reflection and sustainable practices. Philosophers and ethicists continue to explore these challenges, advocating for ethical and sustainable approaches to technological development.

7

Chapter 7: The Impact of Technology on Human Identity

The rapid advancements in digital technology have significantly impacted human identity, reshaping the ways we perceive ourselves and interact with the world. The rise of social media, virtual reality, and artificial intelligence has transformed our sense of self, our relationships, and our societal roles. Philosophers and scholars have explored these changes, examining the implications of technology on human identity and the broader social and cultural consequences.

Social media has profoundly impacted human identity, influencing the ways we present ourselves and interact with others. The curated nature of social media platforms allows individuals to construct and project idealized versions of themselves, blurring the lines between reality and representation. Philosophers like Jean Baudrillard have explored the concept of hyperreality, where the distinction between the real and the simulated becomes increasingly ambiguous. The impact of social media on self-perception, social interactions, and mental health continues to be a significant area of philosophical inquiry.

Virtual reality (VR) and augmented reality (AR) technologies have further transformed our understanding of identity and reality. These technologies create immersive and interactive experiences that challenge traditional notions of space, time, and self. Philosophers like David Chalmers have explored the implications of VR and AR on our understanding of consciousness and existence. The ability to inhabit virtual worlds and interact with digital avatars raises questions about the nature of identity and the potential for new forms of social and cultural interactions.

Artificial intelligence (AI) also plays a significant role in shaping human identity. The development of intelligent machines and digital assistants raises questions about the boundaries between human and machine, as well as the ethical implications of creating entities that mimic human behavior and cognition. Philosophers like Alan Turing and John Searle have explored the nature of artificial intelligence and the ethical considerations of machine consciousness. As AI becomes more integrated into our daily lives, these philosophical inquiries remain crucial in understanding the impact of technology on human identity.

The impact of technology on human identity extends to broader societal and cultural changes. The increasing integration of digital technologies into everyday life has transformed social norms, cultural practices, and economic structures. The digital age has created new opportunities for creativity, innovation, and connectivity, while also presenting challenges related to privacy, security, and ethical responsibility. Philosophers and scholars continue to explore the complex relationship between technology and human identity, providing insights into the broader implications of technological progress.

8

Chapter 8: The Philosophical Implications of Artificial Intelligence

Artificial intelligence (AI) has emerged as one of the most transformative technologies of the digital age, raising profound philosophical questions about the nature of consciousness, intelligence, and human existence. The development of AI has prompted a reevaluation of traditional philosophical concepts and ethical considerations, challenging our understanding of what it means to be human and the role of technology in our lives.

The nature of consciousness is a central philosophical question in the context of AI. Philosophers like René Descartes and David Chalmers have explored the nature of consciousness and the possibility of machine consciousness. The development of AI systems that can perform tasks previously thought to require human intelligence, such as language processing and decision-making, raises questions about the nature of intelligence and the potential for machines to possess consciousness. These philosophical inquiries challenge traditional notions of consciousness and prompt us to consider the ethical implications of creating intelligent machines.

The ethical implications of AI are another critical area of philosophical inquiry. The use of AI in decision-making processes, from healthcare to criminal justice, raises concerns about fairness, accountability, and the potential for bias. Philosophers like John Rawls and Martha Nussbaum have explored the ethical principles of justice and fairness, providing a framework for addressing these challenges. The development and deployment of AI technologies require careful consideration of ethical principles to ensure that they are used responsibly and for the benefit of society.

The potential for AI to surpass human intelligence, known as the technological singularity, also raises profound philosophical and ethical questions. Philosophers like Nick Bostrom have explored the implications of superintelligent AI and the potential risks and benefits associated with its development. The possibility of creating machines that exceed human intelligence prompts us to consider the future of humanity and the role of technology in shaping our destiny. These philosophical inquiries are crucial in guiding the responsible development and use of AI technologies.

9

Chapter 9: The Intersection of Technology and Society

The intersection of technology and society is a complex and dynamic relationship that shapes and is shaped by social, economic, and cultural factors. The digital age has brought unprecedented changes to the way we live, work, and interact, prompting new philosophical and ethical questions about the impact of technology on society. Understanding this intersection requires a multidisciplinary approach, drawing on insights from philosophy, sociology, and other fields.

The impact of technology on social interactions is a significant area of inquiry. The rise of digital communication technologies, such as social media and messaging apps, has transformed the way we connect and communicate with others. Philosophers like Jürgen Habermas have explored the implications of these technologies on public discourse and social interactions. The digital age has created new opportunities for connectivity and community-building, but it has also raised concerns about privacy, surveillance, and the potential for digital divides.

The economic impact of technology is another critical area of inquiry. The digital age has brought significant changes to the global economy, from the rise of the gig economy to the increasing automation of jobs. Philosophers and economists have explored the implications of these changes on labor, income inequality, and economic justice. The digital age presents new challenges and opportunities for economic development, requiring careful consideration of ethical principles and social responsibilities.

The cultural impact of technology is also a critical area of inquiry. The digital age has transformed cultural practices, from the consumption of media and entertainment to the creation of digital art and literature. Philosophers and cultural theorists have explored the implications of these changes on cultural identity and expression. The digital age has created new opportunities for creativity and innovation, but it has also raised questions about cultural preservation and the impact of digital technologies on traditional cultural practices.

10

Chapter 10: The Future of Technology and Human Civilization

As we look to the future, the relationship between technology and human civilization will continue to evolve, presenting new opportunities and challenges. The rapid advancements in digital technology, from artificial intelligence to biotechnology, have the potential to transform every aspect of our lives, from healthcare and education to work and entertainment. Understanding the future of technology and its impact on human civilization requires a multidisciplinary approach, drawing on insights from philosophy, history, and other fields.

The potential for technological advancements to address global challenges is a significant area of inquiry. From climate change and environmental degradation to poverty and disease, technology has the potential to provide innovative solutions to some of the world's most pressing problems. Philosophers and scientists are exploring the ethical and practical implications of using technology to address these challenges, emphasizing the need for responsible and sustainable practices.

The future of work is another critical area of inquiry. The rise of automation and artificial intelligence has the potential to transform labor markets and economic structures, raising questions about the future of employment and economic security. Philosophers and economists are exploring the implications of these changes on labor and income distribution, advocating for policies that promote economic justice and social welfare. The future of work presents new challenges and opportunities, requiring careful consideration of ethical principles and social responsibilities.

The future of human identity and society is also a critical area of inquiry. The digital age has brought unprecedented changes to the way we perceive ourselves and interact with others, raising questions about the future of human relationships and social structures. Philosophers and sociologists are exploring the implications of these changes on identity, community, and social cohesion. The future of human civilization in the digital age requires careful reflection and critical thinking, guided by ethical principles and a commitment to social responsibility.

11

Chapter 11: The Role of Education in the Digital Age

Education plays a crucial role in shaping the future of technology and society. The digital age has brought significant changes to the way we learn and teach, presenting new opportunities and challenges for education. Understanding the role of education in the digital age requires a multidisciplinary approach, drawing on insights from philosophy, pedagogy, and other fields.

The impact of digital technology on education is a significant area of inquiry. The rise of online learning platforms, educational apps, and digital resources has transformed the way we access and engage with knowledge. Philosophers and educators are exploring the implications of these changes on pedagogy, learning outcomes, and educational equity. The digital age presents new opportunities for personalized and accessible education, but it also raises questions about the digital divide and the potential for disparities in educational access and quality.

The ethical implications of digital technology in education are another critical area of inquiry. The use of data and artificial intelligence in educational settings raises concerns about privacy, consent, and the potential for bias. Philosophers and ethicists are exploring the ethical principles of data privacy and fairness, advocating for responsible and ethical use of technology in education. The digital age requires careful consideration of ethical principles to ensure that technology is used to enhance, rather than undermine, educational equity and integrity.

The future of education in the digital age also requires a focus on critical thinking and digital literacy. The rapid advancements in digital technology and the proliferation of information require new skills and competencies for navigating the digital landscape. Philosophers and educators are emphasizing the importance of critical thinking, digital literacy, and ethical reflection in education, advocating for curricula that prepare students for the complexities of the digital age. The future of education requires a commitment to fostering critical and reflective thinkers who can navigate the challenges and opportunities of the digital age.

12

Chapter 12: The Ethical Challenges of Biotechnology

Biotechnology is one of the most promising and controversial fields of technological advancement, raising profound ethical questions about the nature of life, health, and human enhancement. The development of biotechnologies, from genetic engineering to synthetic biology, has the potential to revolutionize healthcare, agriculture, and other fields. Understanding the ethical challenges of biotechnology requires a multidisciplinary approach, drawing on insights from philosophy, bioethics, and other fields.

The ethical implications of genetic engineering are a significant area of inquiry. The ability to manipulate genetic material raises questions about the boundaries of human intervention in nature and the potential for unintended consequences. Philosophers and bioethicists are exploring the ethical principles of autonomy, consent, and justice in the context of genetic engineering, advocating for responsible and ethical practices. The ethical challenges of genetic engineering require careful consideration of the potential risks and benefits, guided by ethical principles and social responsibilities.

The potential for human enhancement through biotechnology also raises profound ethical questions. The development of technologies that can enhance human abilities, from cognitive enhancement to physical augmentation, raises questions about the nature of humanity and the ethical implications of creating "enhanced" individuals. Philosophers and ethicists are exploring the ethical principles of fairness, equality, and the potential for social and economic disparities in the context of human enhancement. The ethical challenges of human enhancement require careful reflection and critical thinking, guided by ethical principles and a commitment to social justice.

The impact of biotechnology on healthcare and public health is another critical area of inquiry. The development of new biotechnologies, from personalized medicine to synthetic biology, has the potential to transform healthcare and improve health outcomes. Philosophers and bioethicists are exploring the ethical principles of beneficence, non-maleficence, and justice in the context of biotechnology and healthcare. The ethical challenges of biotechnology in healthcare require careful consideration of the potential risks and benefits, guided by ethical principles and a commitment to patient welfare.

Chapter 13: The Intersection of Ethics and Emerging Technologies
Emerging technologies, from artificial intelligence to genetic engineering, present new ethical challenges that require careful consideration and critical reflection. The rapid pace of technological advancement raises questions about the ethical implications of these technologies and their impact on society. Philosophers and ethicists are at the forefront of these discussions, exploring the ethical principles and frameworks that can guide the responsible development and use of emerging technologies.

The ethical implications of artificial intelligence are a significant area of inquiry. The development of AI systems that can perform tasks previously thought to require human intelligence raises questions about the nature of intelligence, consciousness, and the potential for machine autonomy. Philosophers and ethicists are exploring the ethical principles of fairness, accountability, and transparency in the context of AI, advocating for responsible and ethical AI development. The ethical challenges of AI require careful reflection on the potential risks and benefits, guided by ethical principles and a commitment to social responsibility.

CHAPTER 12: THE ETHICAL CHALLENGES OF BIOTECHNOLOGY

Genetic engineering is another critical area of ethical inquiry. The ability to manipulate genetic material raises questions about the boundaries of human intervention in nature and the potential for unintended consequences. Philosophers and bioethicists are exploring the ethical principles of autonomy, consent, and justice in the context of genetic engineering, advocating for responsible and ethical practices. The ethical challenges of genetic engineering require careful consideration of the potential risks and benefits, guided by ethical principles and social responsibilities.

The ethical implications of emerging technologies extend to broader societal and environmental impacts. The increasing reliance on digital technologies raises questions about the digital divide, access to technology, and the potential for social and economic inequalities. Additionally, the environmental impact of emerging technologies, from energy consumption to electronic waste, requires ethical reflection and sustainable practices. Philosophers and ethicists continue to explore these challenges, advocating for ethical and sustainable approaches to technological development.

Chapter 14: The Role of Philosophy in Shaping Technological Futures
Philosophy plays a crucial role in shaping the future of technology and society. The philosophical principles and ethical frameworks that guide technological development are essential in ensuring that technology is used responsibly and for the benefit of humanity. Philosophers and ethicists are at the forefront of these discussions, exploring the implications of technological advancements and advocating for ethical and responsible practices.

The philosophical principles of autonomy, justice, and fairness are central to guiding the development and use of technology. The rise of artificial intelligence, genetic engineering, and other emerging technologies raises questions about the ethical implications of these technologies and their impact on society. Philosophers and ethicists are exploring these principles in the context of technological development, advocating for policies and practices that promote ethical and responsible use. The role of philosophy in shaping technological futures is essential in ensuring that technology is used to enhance, rather than undermine, human well-being.

The ethical frameworks that guide technological development are also crucial in addressing the broader societal and environmental implications of technology. The increasing reliance on digital technologies raises questions about the digital divide, access to technology, and the potential for social and economic inequalities. Philosophers and ethicists are exploring these challenges, advocating for ethical and sustainable approaches to technological development. The role of philosophy in shaping technological futures is essential in ensuring that technology is used in ways that promote social justice and environmental sustainability.

The future of technology and society requires a multidisciplinary approach, drawing on insights from philosophy, science, and other fields. The rapid pace of technological advancement presents new opportunities and challenges that require careful reflection and critical thinking. Philosophers and ethicists are at the forefront of these discussions, providing insights and guidance on the ethical and social implications of technology. The role of philosophy in shaping technological futures is essential in ensuring that technology is used to create a better and more just world.

Chapter 15: The Human Element in the Age of Technology The age of technology is not just about machines and algorithms; it is also about the human element. The ways in which we interact with technology, the ethical principles that guide its development, and the societal implications of technological advancements are all fundamentally human concerns. Philosophers, ethicists, and scholars continue to explore the human element in the age of technology, emphasizing the importance of human values, ethics, and social responsibility.

The impact of technology on human relationships and social interactions is a significant area of inquiry. The rise of digital communication technologies, such as social media and messaging apps, has transformed the ways we connect and communicate with others. Philosophers and sociologists are exploring the implications of these technologies on social interactions, privacy, and mental health. The human element in the age of technology requires a focus on fostering meaningful and authentic connections, guided by ethical principles and a commitment to human well-being.

The ethical implications of technology on human life are another critical area of inquiry. The development of artificial intelligence, genetic engineering, and other emerging technologies raises questions about the ethical principles that guide their use and the potential impact on human life. Philosophers and ethicists are exploring these questions, advocating for ethical and responsible practices that prioritize human dignity, autonomy, and well-being. The human element in the age of technology requires a commitment to ethical principles and social responsibility, ensuring that technology is used to enhance, rather than undermine, human life.

The future of technology and society is ultimately shaped by human values and choices. The rapid pace of technological advancement presents new opportunities and challenges that require careful reflection and critical thinking. Philosophers, ethicists, and scholars continue to explore the human element in the age of technology, providing insights and guidance on the ethical and social implications of technological progress. The human element in the age of technology is essential in ensuring that technology is used to create a better and more just world.

The Digital Dialectic: How Philosophy and History Inform the Age of Technology

In "The Digital Dialectic: How Philosophy and History Inform the Age of Technology," readers embark on a captivating journey through the intertwined worlds of philosophy, history, and technology. This thought-provoking book delves into the profound connections between philosophical inquiry and technological innovation, tracing the evolution of human thought and its impact on the digital age.

From the early musings of ancient philosophers to the groundbreaking theories of the Enlightenment, the book explores how philosophical ideas have shaped technological progress throughout history. It examines the symbiotic relationship between philosophy and technology, highlighting how each has influenced and driven the other.

As the narrative unfolds, readers will discover the historical context of technological evolution, from the Industrial Revolution to the digital age. The book provides insights into the ethical dimensions of digital technology, exploring the challenges and opportunities presented by artificial intelligence, genetic engineering, and other emerging technologies.

With a focus on the human element, "The Digital Dialectic" examines the impact of technology on human identity, social interactions, and cultural practices. It raises important philosophical questions about the nature of consciousness, the ethics of machine intelligence, and the future of human-technology interactions.

This comprehensive exploration is not just a reflection on the past but a guide for navigating the complexities of the present and future. By drawing on philosophical principles and historical insights, "The Digital Dialectic" offers readers a deeper understanding of the age of technology and its implications for humanity.

www.ingramcontent.com/pod-product-compliance
Lightning Source LLC
LaVergne TN
LVHW010444070526
838199LV00066B/6181